It was a lover and his lass

Text: Shakespeare

5

Two Eastern Pictures
1. Spring

Text: Kalidasa

GUSTAV HOLST
1874–1934

* Pedal changes for harp.

What ____ sweet voice the

What ____ sweet voice the

B♭ C♮ F♮

cuc - koo's song? ____ Or smil - ing teeth the jas - mine's

cuc - koo's song? ____ Or smil - ing teeth the jas - mine's

C♭ F♯ A♭ B♮

meno mosso

mf

hue? Or ro - sy lips ___ the op - 'ning flowers? ____ Bend - ing

mf

hue? Or ro - sy lips the op - 'ning flowers? ____ Bend - ing

meno mosso

mf

down with blush-ing buds, flam-ing man - go branch-es wave To and fro with the

down with blush-ing buds, flam-ing man - go branch-es wave To and fro with the

B♭

2. Summer

14

16

The graceful swaying wattle

Text: Veronica Mason

FRANK BRIDGE
1879–1941

The bush was grey a week a-go (o - live green, and brown and

The bush was grey a week a-go (o - live green, and brown and

grey), But now the spring has come this way with blos - - som,

grey), But now the spring has come this way with blos - -

blos - som for the wat - tle. __ It seems to be a

- - som for the wat - tle. __ It seems to be a

pow-dery leaves— (the dain · ty, curt-sey-ing wat - tle). _

pow-dery leaves— (the dain - ty, curt-sey-ing wat - tle). _

Its boughs up-lift an el-fin gift, a spray of yel-low

Its boughs up-lift an el-fin gift, a spray of yel-low

down-y drift, Through which the sun-beams shine, and sift their gold dust o'er the

down-y drift, Through which the sun-beams shine, and sift their gold____ dust o'er the

wat - tle. __

wat - tle. __

rall.

rall.

2. Summer

Andante

mm ____ mm ____

The moon shi - neth on yon

mm ____ mm ____

The moon shi - neth on yon

Andante

roof. Here lie maid - ens, crowned with jas - mine, clad ____ in silk

roof. Here lie maid - ens, crowned with jas - mine, clad ____ in silk

rai - ment, on their an - kles are rings that tin - kle sweet - ly as they move.

rai - ment, on their an - kles are rings that tin - kle sweet - ly as they move.

Allegretto

mm ____ mm ____ mm ____ mm ____ mm

Waf - ted by

Allegretto

The lark's grave

Text: Westwood

C. V. STANFORD
1852–1924

The ride of the witch

(The hag)

Text: Robert Herrick

CHARLES WOOD
1866–1926

Mourn no moe

Text: John Fletcher

PETER WARLOCK
1894–1930

Choral Programme Series

Choral repertoire builders with a difference!

Each volume in this new series offers up to 30 minutes of choral music, designed to assist all choirs, large and small, amateur and professional, in imaginative concert programming. Repertoire is drawn from the 18th, 19th and 20th centuries, as well as new commissions, with the emphasis on unavailable, unpublished or unknown material. With expert guidance from Consultant Editor Simon Halsey, maximum practicality is ensured, making the *Choral Programme Series* an invaluable addition to both mixed and upper voice concert repertoire.

The Choral Programme Series

For upper voices:

English Edwardian Partsongs
SSA/piano

Franz Schubert – Three Partsongs
SSAA/piano. Edited by Judith Blezzard

Memory and other choruses from 'Cats'
SSA/piano. Lloyd Webber, arranged by Gwyn Arch

For mixed voices:

Franz Schubert – Four Partsongs
SATB/keyboard. Edited by Judith Blezzard

C.V. Stanford – Seven Partsongs
SATB

Five English Folksongs
SATB. Arranged by Daryl Runswick

Five American Folksongs
SATB. Arranged by Daryl Runswick

Gilbert & Sullivan – Opera Choruses 1
SATB/keyboard. Edited by Ronald Corp

Gilbert & Sullivan – Opera Choruses 2
SATB/keyboard. Edited by Ronald Corp

Antonín Dvořák – Four Choruses for mixed voices Op 29
SATB. Edited by Jan Smaczny

Gustav Holst – Five Partsongs Op 12
SATB

French Chansons – Saint-Saëns/Fauré/Debussy
SATB & SATB/piano. Edited by Timothy Brown

ENGLISH EDWARDIAN PARTSONGS (SA/PIANO & SSA/PIANO)

Faber Music 3 Queen Square London WC1N 3AU

ISBN 0-571-51317-4

9 780571 513178 >